Latimer Study 87

Synods

Gerald Bray

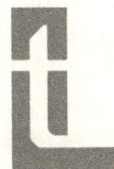

The Latimer Trust

'Synods' © Gerald Bray 2019. All rights reserved.

ISBN 978-1-906327-57-6

Cover photo: 'The Cloister' © by LevT from fotolia.com

Published by the Latimer Trust June 2019.

The Latimer Trust (formerly Latimer House, Oxford) is a conservative Evangelical research organisation within the Church of England, whose main aim is to promote the history and theology of Anglicanism as understood by those in the Reformed tradition. Interested readers are welcome to consult its website for further details of its many activities.

The Latimer Trust

London N14 4PS UK

Registered Charity: 1084337

Company Number: 4104465

Web: www.latimertrust.org

E-mail: administrator@latimertrust.org

Views expressed in works published by The Latimer Trust are those of the authors and do not necessarily represent the official position of The Latimer Trust.

Contents Page

Introduction 1
1. A Brief History of Synodical Government 13
2. General Synod 27
3. Other Synods 49
4. Challenges for the Future 55
5. Evangelicals and Synodical Government 63

1. Introduction

Defining our terms

In modern usage, 'synod' is an ecclesiastical term referring to a gathering of church officers that convenes for the purpose of deliberating what church policy should be. Its agenda may include resolving disputes that have arisen as well as making plans for the future development of the life of the church. Synods are typically representative bodies, though who they represent varies from time to time and from church to church. They have been held from the very earliest days of Christianity, and for many centuries they were understood to be assemblies of bishops. That is still the case in the Roman Catholic and Eastern Orthodox churches, but Protestant practice is much broader in scope. Not all Protestant churches have bishops (or their equivalent), but most distinguish between clergy and laity, both of which are generally represented in their assemblies or synods. It is also generally the case that synods today meet on a regular basis and operate according to a fixed constitution, something that was not true in earlier times.

In the Church of England, synods currently meet at least twice and often three times a year at the national, diocesan and deanery levels, and are composed of roughly equal numbers of clergy and lay people.[1] It must be remembered however that this pattern is a recent one and that it is not necessarily replicated in other churches. Modern English synods share some features in common with those of other times and places, but they are not direct descendants of any particular ancient tradition and have little in common with bodies of the same name that once flourished in the Church. Even before the Reformation, English synods were distinctive because they usually included representatives of the lower clergy along with the bishops, and that pattern has now been extended to embrace the laity as well. It should also be noted that there is no form of Anglican synodical government beyond the level of the

---

[1] Bishops are part of the national and diocesan synods, but not of the deanery ones.

national church, a fact that has become increasingly problematic as the worldwide Anglican Communion has to resolve questions that have arisen because some member churches have acted without consulting the others in ways that can potentially impact the entire Anglican world. It is not too much to say that finding an effective form of synodical government that will be regarded as authoritative by the entire Communion is the greatest challenge facing Anglicans today.[2]

'Synod' was originally a Greek term (*synodos*) that was used in pre-Christian times to denote a gathering or assembly, though nowadays it is reserved exclusively for church affairs. It is sometimes argued that the word's etymology ought to influence its meaning, but this is simplistic. 'Synod' comes from Greek *syn* ('with' or 'together') and *hodos* ('way' or 'road'), but although it clearly means 'a coming together', too much should not be read into that. By the time it entered Christian usage, 'synod' meant no more than 'meeting' or 'assembly'. Its Latin equivalent is *concilium* ('council'),[3] and for a long time the two terms were synonymous. That may still be the case in some contexts, but it is no longer true most of the time. Nowadays, the word 'council' is widely used outside the church to describe a number of different kinds of bodies, only some of which are elected, representative assemblies. A city or county council, for example, will resemble a church synod in that respect, but an organisation like the British Council, which promotes British culture abroad, does not. The Christian world has been influenced by this secular usage, as can be seen from the naming of such bodies as the World Council of Churches and the Anglican Consultative Council, neither of which could be called a 'synod'.

In the traditional ecclesiastical sense of the word, 'council' is now used to refer to the historical ecumenical councils and their successors in the

---

[2] There is a vast and growing literature on this subject. See especially, Paul Valliere, *Conciliarism. A history of decision-making in the Church* (Cambridge: Cambridge University Press, 2012) and Phil Ashey, *Anglican Conciliarism. The Church meeting to decide together* (Newport Beach, CA: Anglican House, 2017).
[3] Often confused, even in medieval times, with *consilium* ('counsel').

INTRODUCTION

Roman Catholic Church, the most recent of which was the Second Vatican Council (1962-65). It is also found at the opposite end of the governmental spectrum, to denote the Parochial Church Council (PCC), an essentially lay body that is normally chaired by the incumbent of a parish and that oversees its everyday operations.[4] The term might conceivably be used to designate a provincial assembly, in which case it is synonymous with 'synod', but this is rare and is usually associated with historical gatherings that no longer take place on a regular basis. This can cause confusion in the Anglican world because the word 'province' has come to be used to define independent national churches, particularly in the Global South. But in England (and also in Ireland, Canada and Australia) the national church has more than one province, though they seldom function independently of each other. Technically, the provinces of Canterbury and York both have a 'provincial synod' or 'council', but this seldom meets as an independent body and its traditional functions are now largely subsumed into the General Synod, which represents the entire Church. On the other hand, provincial synods do have a life of their own in Australia and the practice could be revived in England if it were ever felt to be desirable to do so.[5]

Modern Anglican synods are also characterised by having a constitutional place in national or regional churches, and their decisions can have (or can acquire) binding force within them. However, there are other gatherings that have some importance in the life of the church even though they lack the same kind of authority, and for these, different terms are used in order to avoid confusion. In the Anglican context, the most obvious one of these is the 'conference', a word that is used to describe the periodic meeting of the bishops of the Anglican Communion at Lambeth. 'Assembly' is the term preferred by the World Council of Churches for its periodic meetings, while the Episcopal Church in the United States has a triennial General Convention.

---

[4] These councils replace the older parish vestries, a term that is still often found in other Anglican churches.
[5] The English provincial synods are the same as the convocations (see below) which do not include the laity. There are no provincial synods in England that correspond to the current national or diocesan pattern of lay inclusion.

More recently the word 'council' has been pressed into service to describe the Primates' Council, an essentially informal gathering of the primates of the autonomous Anglican churches around the world that meets from time to time. Some have suggested that it might evolve into a pan-Anglican synod, but that has not happened yet and is probably unlikely, not least because of its overly restricted and unrepresentative character.

The current situation, as far as synods are concerned, can be summarised as follows:

1. Synods and councils were originally the same thing, but although the two terms can still be occasionally synonymous, for most purposes they have become differentiated in modern times.

2. The word 'synod' now refers to a representative body within the Church that possesses some form of legislative or regulatory authority and therefore functions as part of the Church's internal administration.

3. The word 'synod' (though not 'council') is reserved for gatherings that transcend the local parish or benefice and that include both clergy and laity. In the Church of England these synods meet at the levels of the rural (area) deanery, the diocese and the nation as a whole, but not at the level of the province.

The New Testament evidence for synods

The Church has always claimed to base its organisational structure on the evidence of the New Testament, even though that evidence is patchy and susceptible to different interpretations. What is certain is that from the very beginning the Church had a collective leadership structure that can be traced back to Jesus himself. During his earthly ministry there was no 'church' as we now understand it, and his absolute leadership was never questioned by his followers. But Jesus chose twelve men to be his disciples, of whom three (Peter, James and John) appear to have formed an inner circle of some kind. After his resurrection it was this group of twelve (minus Judas, who was replaced by the election of

Introduction

Matthias, recorded in Acts 1:23-26) that formed the core of what was soon to become a rapidly expanding church. Despite the claim to the contrary that is put forward by the Roman Catholic Church today, there is no real evidence that Peter occupied a special position among these disciples, who were henceforth known as apostles. It is true that Jesus gave Peter the so-called 'keys of the kingdom' (Matthew 16:19) but as he gave the same authority to the disciples as a whole (Matthew 18:18; John 20:23) this text cannot be used to claim that Peter was somehow greater than the others.

It is also true that Peter was the spokesman for the apostles on the day of Pentecost (Acts 2:14-42) but the text makes it clear that he preached in association with the others and that it was their collective teaching that the 3000 new converts were called to embrace. Later on, when Paul was welcomed into the apostolic circle, he touched base with Peter (Galatians 1:18) but he also made the acquaintance of James at the same time. More significantly, Paul denied that his apostolic commission came from the others, and if he recognised Peter in any special way it was only as the apostle to the Jews, in contrast to his own commission, which was to go to the Gentiles (Galatians 2:8). Most importantly of all, Paul's mission was approved by James (mentioned first, perhaps because he was the head of the Jerusalem church), Peter and John, whom he described as being the chief apostles, another sign that the leadership, even in Jerusalem, was collective in nature and not entrusted to Peter (or James) individually. As far as we know, Paul always dealt with the Jerusalem church as a body and never considered that there was one person who could speak for it with an authority that the others did not possess.

We do not know how this collective leadership worked in practice, but there is no doubt that it did, as we can see from the events recorded in Acts 15. The church in Antioch had been troubled by certain visitors from Jerusalem who tried to insist that the Gentile converts made in the Syrian capital had to become Jews if they wanted to be Christians. This meant that the men had to be circumcised and probably also that they all had to follow Jewish dietary laws. (That is not explicitly stated in the text but it may be inferred from the decisions that were eventually taken with respect to them.) In order to resolve the crisis which this intervention caused, the Antiochene church despatched Paul, Barnabas and some others to confer with the leaders in Jerusalem. When they got there, they formed an assembly that may justly be called the first recorded synod of the Church as a whole.

The first thing to notice about this synod is its *composition*. It did not consist of every member of either the Antiochene or the Jerusalem church, but of designated representatives from each. This was an obvious necessity in the case of the Antiochenes, since it was hardly possible for the entire church to decamp to Jerusalem, but it is noteworthy that those who went had the support of their sending congregation and a clear brief from it as to what was expected of them. In Jerusalem, it seems that everyone turned out to greet the delegates when they arrived, but the discussions themselves were carried on by the apostles and the elders of the church, not by the membership as a whole (Acts 15:6). Whether these representatives can be equated with the bishops and presbyters (priests) of later times is debatable, but there is no doubt that those involved in the synod were there because of their recognised status within the Jerusalem community. They were not specially chosen delegates but neither were they people who had no wider responsibilities, so it may be assumed that their decisions carried some authority, and that they would be implemented once the synod was over.

The second thing to notice is that there was a *long discussion* about the question at issue. From our point of view it may seem that the conclusion was never in doubt, but that was not obvious to the participants at the time. There must have been real questions that demanded serious debate, since otherwise the amount of time devoted to them would have been disproportionate. We can probably assume that the Antiochenes were all on one side of the argument and that the dissenting voices came from the Jerusalem side, but they were taken seriously and there is no suggestion that those whose opinions were overruled were ejected from the Church as heretics.

The third thing to notice is that *agreement was reached* when the leaders of the Jerusalem church persuaded their own colleagues that the Antiochenes were basically right. Peter spoke from his own experience. He had ministered to Gentiles and had seen how the Holy Spirit had worked in them just as he had worked in Jewish converts. The apostolic preaching had borne fruit in exactly the same way and there was therefore no reason to suppose that the conversion of the Gentiles was somehow defective. James continued the argument by appealing to Scripture. What the church was witnessing was the fulfilment of what the prophet Amos had long ago predicted (Amos 9:11-12). This was fully in line with the belief that the Pentecostal outpouring was the outworking of ancient Jewish prophecy, as indeed was the entire Gospel. Biblical teaching thus combined with empirical evidence to win the case for Gentile inclusion in the church, without the need to adopt Judaism in the process.

The fourth thing to notice is that *the views of the minority were not ignored* or overruled. The Gentiles may have been in the right in principle, but in deference to Jewish sensitivities they were asked not to eat meat that had been sacrificed to idols, not to engage in sexual immorality (also associated with pagan worship) and not to eat the meat of animals that had been strangled and that still contained their blood. The first and third of these were concessions to the law of Moses that did not violate the basic principle of Gentile inclusion but that had come to be expected of believers because of the way in which the law had been regularly preached in the synagogues for longer than anyone could remember. We know from other parts of the New Testament that there were 'weaker brethren' in the churches who were upset by Gentiles who ignored these restrictions, but while Paul agreed that the Gentiles were theoretically correct, he upheld the decisions of the Jerusalem synod as a matter of courtesy and love towards those who found it hard to accept the new dispensation (1 Corinthians 8:1-13; Romans 14:13-23).

The fifth thing to notice about the Jerusalem synod was that its *decisions were recorded in writing* and backed up by a delegation from Jerusalem that accompanied the Antiochenes on their return home.

This was to ensure that the Gentiles in Antioch would know that the measures taken (largely in their favour) were real and that the Jerusalem church would abide by them. No doubt Paul and Barnabas would have reported what had happened, but their word on its own was not enough. There had to be some objective confirmation of the synod's action that could be used in case of any future doubt or objection that might be raised. In this respect we might add that Luke's account in Acts 15 is further evidence of what transpired, and that it continues to guide our thinking today, long after the letter sent by the Jerusalem church to Antioch has disappeared. What was determined by two local churches thus became normative for the Christian world as a whole, even though nobody else took part in the discussions.[6] In this respect at least, the Jerusalem synod had, and continues to have, an authoritative status that no subsequent synod can claim – an important point, to the implications of which we shall return.

There is no other meeting recorded in the New Testament that was of similar importance to the Jerusalem synod. There is ample evidence that apostles like Paul and John exercised an authority over churches, including ones that they had not founded, but this authority derived from their apostleship, which obviated the need for further synods. Scholars debate whether there were competing Pauline and Johannine churches (at Ephesus, for example), but there is no real evidence for that hypothesis and the writings of both men were incorporated into the New Testament without dissent. Synods were not called in the apostolic age because they were not necessary as long as the Church was small and cohesive enough for disputes to be settled without too much acrimony. Somewhat amazingly, this situation seems to have continued for the next two centuries, surviving both the rise of heretical movements and the dangers incurred by both the uncontrolled expansion and the increasingly widespread persecution of the Church.

---

[6] There seems to be some recognition that the Jerusalem church had a prestige that set it apart from the others and that if it approved of something, then its decisions had to be taken seriously elsewhere. If the Jerusalem church did in fact occupy such a position, it lost it after the destruction of Jerusalem in AD 70 and there is no evidence that its special role was taken over by any other church.

Despite everything, believers held together and when the synodical structure re-emerged in the third century it did so in a climate where apostolic authority, now mediated through the New Testament Scriptures, continued to command the assent of all who called themselves Christians.

The relevance of New Testament principles today

To what extent and in what way can the Jerusalem synod serve as an ongoing model for the Church today? At one level, it is clear that the problems it dealt with are no longer current. No church nowadays has to face a core of Jewish believers who object to the admission of Gentiles, and it is almost impossible to imagine that such a situation could ever recur. Even Messianic Jews, Christian converts from Judaism who continue to observe Jewish customs, do not attempt to impose them on others and nobody would take them seriously if they did. The significance of the Jerusalem synod for us today must therefore be sought in the underlying principles that governed its behaviour rather than in the actual details recorded in Acts 15. These principles can be outlined as follows:

1. It is legitimate for the church to entrust decision-making to elected representatives, and to expect that those representatives will have wider responsibilities in the church that will ensure that they will have to live with their decisions and apply them. The orderly conduct of business will require chairmanship, and that may be placed in the hands of a particular individual (like the archbishop of Canterbury, for example), but that role must not become a form of dictatorship in the way that the papacy has often been in the Roman Catholic Church. Not even the most exalted church dignitary is infallible, and every synod must accept the possibility that it may have taken the wrong decision. If it has, the solution is for a subsequent synod to put matters right, and it is not for one individual, however important or gifted he may be, to determine the outcome on his own.

2. It is right for contentious issues to be properly debated and for a generally acceptable consensus to be sought. That consensus need not

be 'pure' in the sense that it may require some theoretically unnecessary concessions to be made, but as long as fundamental Gospel principles are not compromised, that is a price worth paying for the sake of harmony within the body of Christ. This can be seen today in the provision made for those who cannot accept certain forms of ministry being exercised by a woman. The women concerned may be unhappy about this arrangement but it is not for them (or their male supporters) to impose what is essentially a new practice on those who are not prepared to receive it.

3. Those in positions of leadership must lead, and they must do so by relying on Biblical teaching and the way that this has worked out in practice. Quoting the Bible in the abstract is not enough, because verses can easily be taken out of context and twisted. At the same time, the appeal to experience is not enough either, since it may be no more than a corrupt tradition that has been allowed to develop unchecked. Principles and practice must go together and reinforce one another. For this to work properly it is necessary for the voices of those who have the requisite knowledge and experience to be heard. Synods are a place for mature deliberation, and while the contribution of young radicals should not be dismissed, neither should it be allowed to set the agenda as if ignoring the lessons of the past were the incontrovertible way ahead for the future.

4. Conservative minorities must not be ignored when changes are proposed. One area in which this has immediate and obvious application is in church worship. When new liturgies are introduced the old ones should not simply be abolished, as long as there are people attached to them. They may fall into disuse over time, but that process should be a natural one and not something imposed by majority vote, against the wishes of a significant minority. Traditionalists are not heretics *per se*, and should not be treated as if they were.

5. Synodical decisions must be clearly stated and explained to the wider church. Uncertainty about what was 'really' decided or failure to communicate the decisions properly can only lead to confusion,

discontent and (perhaps) further division, making the latter state worse than the first. Synods are representative bodies and therefore they must account for their actions to those whom they represent. If they fail to do so, their legitimacy will be questioned and the role that they are called to perform will be compromised.

2. A Brief History of Synodical Government

From ancient times to the Reformation

The first post-Biblical synods of which we have any real knowledge date from the mid to late third century. Most of them were concerned with problems arising from the election of bishops in different churches. It sometimes happened that rival candidates would provoke a schism rather than defer to someone else, and in a situation like that it was necessary to call together bishops from neighbouring churches who would arbitrate the dispute. Occasionally doctrinal issues would also surface, as they apparently did in Antioch in 268, when its bishop, Paul of Samosata, was deposed for preaching the heresy of adoptionism. Whether this was true, or just an excuse to get rid of the unpopular Paul, is not clear, but the incident shows that synods were expected to pronounce on matters of doctrine if they were required to do so, as well as to resolve what were essentially disciplinary disputes.

Synods came into their own after the legalisation of Christianity in AD 313. We know that a number of them were held throughout the fourth and fifth centuries, and some provinces of the Roman Empire developed a local synodical tradition that continued for a long time. In North Africa, for example, synods were held regularly until the Vandal conquest in AD 430. In Gaul (France) there was a similar trend that lasted into the sixth century. Most famous of all were the seventeen councils of Toledo, held between 400 and the Arab conquest of Spain in 711, which developed a whole series of disciplinary regulations that later found their way into the canon law of the Western (Roman) church. In addition to these provincial synods, there was also a series of imperial ('ecumenical') councils that met periodically to determine what the church's official doctrine should be. The first of these was held at Nicaea in 325, the second at Constantinople in 381, the third at Ephesus in 431 and the fourth at Chalcedon, a suburb of Constantinople, in 451. These were the four ancient ecumenical councils that were officially recognised in later times and whose decisions the Church of England continues to accept today, but there were others, like the second council of Ephesus in 449, which were repudiated because a majority of the attendees voted for false doctrine. That too, is important to remember, because the truth or falsity of a belief was not determined by synodical vote but by an appeal to the Scriptures and the wider tradition of the church.

After the collapse of the Roman Empire in the West it became more difficult to hold synods, but they continued in the East until the late ninth century. The last one to receive universal recognition was the second council of Nicaea (787), which was also the seventh 'ecumenical' council, but there were later ones in 870 and 880 that were held in Constantinople and whose exact status is uncertain. The problem with them is that Rome and the West recognise the first of these (which deposed Photius, the patriarch of the imperial capital) and the East recognises the second (which reinstated him!)

After that, there was a long pause before more 'ecumenical' councils were summoned, but by the time they were revived it was the pope rather than the emperor who called them. There was a famous series of four councils held in the Lateran Palace in Rome from 1123 to 1215 that settled the canon law of the Western church and whose decisions retain some of their importance even now. The reading of the banns of marriage, for example, dates from the Fourth Lateran Council in 1215, as does the official acceptance of the Roman Catholic doctrine of transubstantiation. For the next 200 years or more, councils were held away from Rome, in places like Lyon (1245 and 1274), Vienne (1313), Constance (1414-1417) and Basel (1436). The last of these was an attempt to decentralise the Western church by making the pope more of a figurehead and devolving real power to the council itself, but the papacy was eventually able to outwit the so-called 'conciliarists'. Armed with a promise of reunion with the Eastern churches, Pope Eugenius IV was able to transfer the council from Basel to Ferrara and then to Florence when Ferrara was struck with the plague. It is now generally known as the Council of Florence (1439) but it was eventually transferred to Rome, where it was wound up in 1444. After that there was one more medieval council, Lateran V (1512-1517), which tried to tackle the much-needed reform of the church but failed to make much headway. It ended only a few months before Martin Luther posted his Ninety-five Theses on the church door in Wittenberg.

Since the Reformation, the Roman Catholic Church has held three 'ecumenical' councils, one at Trent (1545-1563) and two at the Vatican, the first in 1870 and the second in 1962-1965. Trent is famous for having established modern ('Counter-Reformation') Catholicism, Vatican I saw the proclamation of papal infallibility and Vatican II has become the springboard and reference point for the modern reforms of the Roman Church. Needless to say, none of these later councils is recognised by the Anglican or other Protestant churches, although they all participated to some extent as observers at Vatican II. In the current ecumenical climate of opinion it is hard to see how the Roman Church could call another council without involving the wider Christian world, but whether it will or not remains to be seen. In the meantime, papal centralisation of the Church is such that provincial, diocesan and other local synods, while they exist, have little to do other than tackle purely local problems. The various Eastern Orthodox churches also have their local synods, which meet on a regular basis, but they have never managed to convene a gathering of the entire Orthodox world. Attempts to do so are constantly being made but so far they have failed to materialise.[1]

One important point to bear in mind is that Roman Catholic and Eastern Orthodox synods, like those held in ancient times, are meetings of bishops only, who represent their local dioceses. Neither the lower clergy nor the laity are invited. The Protestant world is very different. From the beginning of the Reformation, Protestant church synods have embraced the lower clergy, who were often the only ones left after the episcopate was abolished. Lay representation has been patchier, but in the sixteenth century secular rulers and parliaments represented the lay interest and the clergy were seldom able to act without them. In many

---

[1] A Holy and Great Council of the Orthodox Churches met from 19-26 June 2016 on Crete, but four (of fourteen) national churches boycotted it. Even so, it was a historic first in the Orthodox world and may be the beginning of more such councils to come.

cases, the boot was very much on the other foot, with the clergy having to do as the secular rulers told them. The situation varied enormously from one place to another, but state (and therefore lay) control was the order of the day in the Protestant world.[2] In general, it can be said that Reformed (Calvinist) churches did better in this respect than Lutheran ones, which often became little more than departments of state. The Reformed were able to call an international synod at Dordrecht (Dort) in Holland, which met over the winter of 1618-1619 and framed what are now called the 'five points of Calvinism'. The French Protestant Church was forbidden to send delegates to Dort but it was allowed to hold its own synods, which met regularly from 1559 to 1659, after which restrictions were placed on them until the church itself was dissolved in 1685.

In the British Isles, the Church of Scotland established a General Assembly which, with a few interruptions, has met annually from 1560 until the present time. Serving a Presbyterian church, the General Assembly contains both clergy and lay people, a pattern that is repeated throughout the Reformed world.

Synods in the Church of England

The history of synods in the Church of England goes back to its origins in the seventh century. In Anglo-Saxon times synods or councils were held at periodic intervals, and for the most part they represented the national church, insofar as there was such a thing. Until the tenth century England was divided into a number of small kingdoms, and the Church was the only truly 'national' institution. As was the case elsewhere in the West, the synods were meetings of bishops presided over by the metropolitan, who was the archbishop of Canterbury. Technically this was a provincial synod that should have had a counterpart in York, but that subtlety seems to have been overlooked most of the time. Basically, the Anglo-Saxon church was not well-

---

[2] Roman Catholic clergy and their Eastern Orthodox counterparts were by no means shielded from lay involvement in their affairs, but that pressure was never institutionalised in the way that it was in the Protestant world.

organised because there was nobody with enough power and authority to organise it. The papacy was weak and far away, dioceses were based on ancient tribal divisions more than anything else, and the kings of England, even after the country was united in the reign of Athelstan (927-940), were usually too weak to do much about it.

The Norman conquest changed everything. The papacy was already reforming itself and the popes agreed to support William the Conqueror as long as he promised to put the English Church in order. This William agreed to do, but it took longer than he might have expected. Within a century however, the dioceses had been rearranged and parishes had been created along lines already familiar on the continent. Bishops, who in Anglo-Saxon times had sat in the king's courts alongside other nobles, were set apart and the rudiments of a separate church administration were established. Synodical government would follow in due course, this time along clearly delimited provincial and diocesan lines.

By the late thirteenth century the system was well established and functioning, but the emergence of parliament presented a new challenge. What role should the Church play in it and how would the new secular body relate to the Church? From the king's point of view, the most important thing was taxation. The clergy could not be taxed in the same way as the laity, but the Church was too wealthy to be left to its own devices. A special form of clerical taxation had to be devised, camouflaged as a 'benevolence' or 'free gift' that the Church supposedly offered to the crown. To obtain this money, the king issued writs to the archbishops, advising them to summon their provincial synods for the purpose of granting money to the king. Because of the nature of the request, these provincial synods were not strictly comparable to the episcopal assemblies that had become traditional elsewhere. Instead, they consisted not only of bishops but of the abbots of the leading monasteries who also possessed land and had a lot of taxable revenue, together with selected members of the lower clergy. The deans and representatives of cathedral chapters were summoned to attend, as were the archdeacons and two representatives from the beneficed clergy.

Alongside them there was also an assortment of clerics from various 'peculiar jurisdictions' that lay outside the diocesan system but that were often wealthy in their own right. There were only a few of these in the province of Canterbury but there were more in York, where the archbishop and the bishop of Durham almost went around collecting them. Huge tracts of Yorkshire, including Howden and Northallerton, thus found themselves represented in these clerical assemblies even though, as peculiar jurisdictions, they had no official standing in the church hierarchy.

Over time this gathering of clergy, summoned by royal writ for the purpose of taxation, came to be called a 'convocation', the name which is preserved to this day for the clerical members of the General Synod. The convocations were provincial synods because they were summoned by the archbishops, but the latter also had the power to summon their clergy independently of the king, in which case the gathering would not be a 'convocation' in the official sense. However, lines were soon blurred, and by 1400 the difference between the two bodies was rapidly being forgotten. One reason for this is that the Hundred Years' War with France was consuming a vast amount of the national treasure, with the result that Richard II (1377-1399) was summoning convocations all the time. A provincial synod that was *not* a convocation would have been very hard to fit into the schedule! There were even occasions when the king got wind of a provincial synod being held and wrote to it asking for a benevolence, thereby turning the gathering into a tax convocation.

At the same time, the rise of Lollardy made the convening of provincial synods more urgent and the early fifteenth century saw them engaging in doctrinal matters to a degree that had previously been unknown in England. The Europe-wide conciliar movement was also in full swing at this time, and the English Church played a part in it, sending delegates to the continent on a regular basis.[3] This period of frenetic synodal

---

[3] The conciliar movement was an attempt to dilute the authority of the papacy by subjecting the popes to church councils that would meet every five years or so. It arose out of attempts to resolve the great schism of the papacy, which produced two and even three popes between 1378 and 1417.

activity died down in the second half of the fifteenth century, partly because conciliarism was defeated and partly because England was no longer constantly at war with France, but mainly because the monarchy was going through a crisis of its own, known to us as the Wars of the Roses. Those wars finally ended when Henry VII came to the throne in 1485, after which things settled down once more.

Lasting change came with Henry VIII (1509-1547). The archbishop of Canterbury summoned what would turn out to be the last independent provincial synod in 1510, and the archbishop of York did the same in 1515, though his synod never actually met. The archbishop who summoned it was none other than Thomas Wolsey, who soon became the king's first minister and a cardinal of the Roman Church. Wolsey was a reformer who wanted to merge the two provinces of the English Church into one by creating a single national synod that would legislate for both provinces. He succeeded briefly in 1523 by using his legatine powers as the pope's representative in England, in order to override the objections of the archbishop of Canterbury. It was a shortlived success though, because once the Church of England broke with Rome, institutional reform of the kind envisaged by Wolsey was effectively abandoned. The convocations were subjected to the authority of the king, and although there was a renewed attempt to merge them in 1540, it did not work. The only real change was that from 1545 onwards, the convocations would be summoned to meet in tandem with Parliament, an arrangement that was to last until 1966.

There were two major problems with this system, neither of which was ever solved. The first was that the two convocations differed enormously in size. Canterbury had twenty-one dioceses but York had only five, one of which was the minuscule diocese of Sodor and Man which lay outside the Kingdom of England and did not really count. The other was that the bishops all sat in the House of Lords, making their simultaneous appearance in convocation difficult, and in the case of York, impossible.[4] This made meaningful deliberation very rare and did much

---

[4] The bishop of Sodor and Man sat (and still sits) in Tynwald, the island's parliament, and not in the House of Lords.

to transfer ecclesiastical business to Parliament, where it could be debated and decided on a national basis.

The sixteenth-century reforms meant that the convocations would be kept in being whenever Parliament was sitting. Despite the problems this caused, they were still able to transact business and they did so, producing a large corpus of canon law, doctrinal statements and prayer books for the Reformed Church. However, in order for these things to become law they had to receive the royal assent, which Queen Elizabeth I (1558-1603) was slow to grant. As the epic struggle between crown and Parliament got underway in the seventeenth century, one of the claims advanced by the latter was that the convocations were subordinate not only to the monarch, but to the Parliament as well, a proposition that both the king and most of the bishops denied. The ambiguity of this situation was exposed, to cruel effect, when Charles I (1625-1649) believed that he could approve ecclesiastical legislation, and incidentally tax the clergy, independently of Parliament, but his attempt to do so in 1640 precipitated civil war and the destruction of both the crown and the Church in its traditional form. Parliament replaced the convocations by the Westminster Assembly, which operated along similar lines but included Scotland and Ireland in its remit as well as Canterbury and York. The Westminster Assembly was free to act in Church affairs but Parliament was reluctant to turn its decisions into law and the new experiment in Church government ended in failure.

The old system was officially restored in 1660, but it never really recovered. The Church gave up its independent taxation in 1663, just after composing a new Prayer Book that Parliament had to approve before it could become law. After that there was little point in summoning the convocations and they went into long-term decline. York virtually disappeared altogether, but Canterbury was revived from 1701 to 1717. Unfortunately the convocation spent most of its time battling over the rights of the lower clergy *versus* the bishops, which was a political issue more than anything else, and very little was accomplished. The bishops were all appointees of the revolutionary (post-1688) administration, whereas most of the lower clergy were reactionaries who were sympathetic to Jacobitism, even if they could not say so openly. They wanted to recover their right to a separate taxation but this was denied them, so they spent their time denouncing Deistic heretics that they uncovered in the universities. The convocation enjoyed the patronage of Queen Anne (1702-1714), especially after 1709, but its arch-conservatism made it unpalatable to the Hanoverian George I, who soon found an excuse to suspend its sessions.

From 1717 to 1852 the convocations existed only in a formal sense. They were duly elected every time there was a new Parliament and the Canterbury one then presented a loyal address to the king, after which it effectively ceased to function.[5] York did nothing at all. It was only in 1852, when pressure on the Church from a rapidly secularising state made it necessary to re-establish some form of independent government, that Lord Aberdeen, the prime minister of the day, allowed the convocation of Canterbury to meet to transact business once more. York dragged its feet because its archbishop was hostile to the move, and it was not until 1861 that it finally followed suit.

The re-emergence of the two provincial convocations as functioning legislative bodies created two problems that the Church had to resolve. The first was to do with Ireland. The Church of Ireland had been united with the Church of England in 1801, but its convocation had not met for some years and was effectively abandoned. In any case, it had been a national, not a provincial body, and so did not fit the English pattern. But after 1852 the danger was that the Irish Church would be forced to accept decisions approved by Canterbury (and eventually by York) without having a say in framing them. Efforts were therefore made to revive the Irish convocation but these failed, and the opportunity was taken by the state to separate the two churches and to disestablish the Church of Ireland altogether. The newly disestablished Church was thus able (and effectively forced) to develop its own administrative structure, which it did by creating a General Synod that met for the first time in

---

[5] There was a brief exception in 1741 and for a time it looked as though the convocations might be revived, but the bishops concluded that they were not necessary and they sank back into the doldrums.

1870. Despite all the troubles in Ireland since that time, the General Synod continues to meet and must be regarded as a success. It consists of three houses – bishops, clergy representatives and lay delegates – and meets annually in May or June. Most importantly, for our present purposes, it provided a model for other Anglican churches, and eventually even the Church of England, to follow in due course. The creation of an English General Synod was not the inevitable result of a disestablishment that has not occurred, but it was the fruit of a growing separation between Church and state which made it both desirable and necessary for the Church to have greater autonomy in managing its affairs.

The other big problem which the Church of England faced when the convocations were revived was the lack of lay representation in them. They had been designed to give the clergy a certain identity and independence within the tax system, and although that purpose was no longer relevant, their character had hardly changed. The monasteries had disappeared of course, and following reforms in the 1830s and 1840s the peculiar jurisdictions were greatly reduced in number, but otherwise they retained the flavour of a bygone era. At least some of the objections raised to their revival had to do with this – they were no longer fit for purpose and if they were not adapted to meet the new conditions that the Church was facing they might easily do more harm than good. The lay element, previously represented by Parliament, could no longer function as it had done once Parliament was open to non-Anglicans, so something new had to be devised. This was a 'House of Laity' which was set up in 1885 on a purely informal basis. Only the convocations had voting rights, and although the lay viewpoint might be taken into consideration as a matter of courtesy, there was no obligation on anyone to take it seriously.

This situation was obviously unsatisfactory, but it was not until 1919 that something was done about it. By then, the Welsh dioceses of the Church were about to be disestablished and so they were excluded from the new arrangements. The remaining Church of England was reorganised by the creation of a National Assembly that combined the two convocations with the House of Laity. They met for joint discussions but continued to vote separately, an odd arrangement that nevertheless managed to survive for half a century. In 1970 this National Assembly was finally replaced by the General Synod, which now meets for a fixed five-year term. The General Synod differs from the old Assembly because the voting is by houses, not by provinces, and all three meet together, though the houses may still vote separately if requested to do so.

There is no longer any real difference between the clergy and the laity, though the old (and exclusively clerical) convocations survive in name and some of their traditions are preserved. There is a very limited amount of business that concerns only the clergy and that is dealt with by convening the convocations without the house of laity, but such meetings are rare. As for traditions, the leaders of the house of clergy are called the prolocutors of Canterbury and York, a title that preserves the ancient name for their speakers, and the members of the house are styled 'proctors', as they have been since medieval times. There is also a convocation sermon at the start of each new General Synod, a tradition that likewise goes back to the middle ages, and a loyal address to the crown that the Canterbury convocation first made in 1689. But apart from symbolic forms like these, the General Synod is a new creation whose relationship to its predecessors is more superficial than real.

As far as other synods are concerned, diocesan ones can be traced back to the middle ages but it is not clear that they did much back then. They seem to have been annual meetings of the clergy when they received the chrism needed for baptisms at Easter and heard the bishop or his representative give a kind of 'state of the diocese' address. Very little is known about them and, as far as we can tell, they did virtually nothing. The one exception to this rule was the diocese of Sodor and Man, which since 1704 has possessed its own convocation that has met in tandem with Tynwald, the island's parliament. Since 1970 Sodor and Man has had a diocesan synod and its ancient convocation, while still in existence, is a shadow of its former self, but although it was never called a diocesan synod, that is in fact what it was, and its records give us a fascinating picture of how a diocese actually functioned in the eighteenth and nineteenth centuries. Otherwise, it has to be said that modern diocesan synods are more like miniature versions of the General Synod than like their medieval predecessors, which can be ignored for our purposes. Deanery synods do not seem to have existed in earlier times, and deaneries themselves virtually disappeared for several centuries. They were revived in the mid-nineteenth century, more or less at the same time as the convocations, but they did not have a functioning synodical government of their own until 1970.

The current system of synodical government in the Church of England is now half a century old, but in some respects it is still in the process of formation. Its membership has been altered in recent years, mainly with a view towards slimming it down in order to save money, and its relationship to Parliament is still a work in progress. Since 1919 Parliament has passed fewer statutes for the Church, but it continues to legislate for it in the form of 'measures' which have the same force in law. These measures are drafted by the Church and passed by the General Synod (or by the National Assembly before 1970) and then sent to Parliament for ratification. Most of the time this is granted without much debate, but that cannot be guaranteed. In 1928, for example, Parliament threw out the measure for Prayer Book revision, despite the fact that it had been passed by both convocations, and more recently, the Churchwardens Measure (2001) was delayed for several years because Parliament was not satisfied that the traditional rights of churchwardens were being given adequate protection.

On both these occasions there was considerable resentment in some Church circles at what was seen as parliamentary 'interference' in the Church's business, but Parliament was exercising its rights, and it may do so again in future. It is possible that at some point this delicate relationship will produce a crisis that will lead to disestablishment, but so far that has been avoided and there is nothing on the horizon that would make such a development likely. However the future is unpredictable and it is by no means impossible that something like that will happen, perhaps unexpectedly and in circumstances that nobody particularly wants. For the time being, disestablishment is a dormant issue but if that were to change, then the General Synod would undoubtedly become the mechanism for administering the newly independent Church of England. Its present constitution might be revised to some extent to meet the new circumstances, but in all probability that modification would be minimal, because of the need to preserve as much continuity as possible in a time of upheaval. For that reason, if for no other, its constitution and procedures are important and must be understood by everyone concerned with the Church's affairs today.

As set up in 1970, General Synod is elected for a five-year term, but this is fixed and is no longer concurrent with Parliament. Casual vacancies within the first two years are filled by recounting the votes, excluding the candidate who has resigned and protecting those already elected. After two years there is a by-election. Vacancies occur with some regularity, especially in the house of clergy, since proctors must vacate their seat if they leave the diocese they represent. As a result, many of those who lost out in the general election will eventually be seated in the Synod, as long as they have remained in the same diocese. Those who stay put may serve as long as they are re-elected, which in some cases may be for thirty years or more. In that respect, General Synod is similar to Parliament, and multiple terms are common, giving the Synod the benefit (or the burden?) of the experience gained from longevity of service and compensating to some extent for the removal of most of the traditional *ex officio* posts, especially in the house of clergy.

3. General Synod

Composition

The current General Synod of the Church of England consists of three houses – bishops, clergy and laity. Of these, the house of bishops is the most 'representative' and the house of laity the least, but that is only to be expected, given the respective numbers of each. The important point is that no house is fully inclusive of its potential membership, and only the house of clergy can be called 'democratic' in the sense that this is generally understood by wider society.

The house of bishops embraces all diocesan bishops in the Church, including those of Sodor and Man and of Europe, which lie outside England and whose incumbents do not have the right to sit in the House of Lords.[1] In addition to the diocesans, there is a small representation of suffragan bishops (five from Canterbury and four from York), who are elected by their peers. Retired bishops cannot sit in the General Synod, nor is the house open to overseas bishops who have entered (or more usually re-entered) the Church of England's ministry in another capacity.[2]

---

[1] When new dioceses were created after 1836, episcopal representation in the House of Lords was frozen at the then existing number of twenty-six. The five senior sees (Canterbury, York, London, Durham and Winchester) are always represented and the remaining twenty-one are seated in order of seniority. However, for a decade from 18 May 2015, this order is being interrupted in favour of advancing female bishops ahead of their male colleagues. The old system will be restored in 2025. It may also be noted that any clergyman (or woman) who is a peer may sit in the House of Lords without being a bishop.
[2] There is a small number of English clergy who have gone abroad and served as bishops in other Anglican churches before returning home to take a parish, but although the Church recognises their episcopal orders and may grant them the right to perform some episcopal functions, they do not belong to the English episcopate. Whether someone like that could be elected to serve in the house of clergy is a moot point – the most that can be said about that is that it has not (so far) been tested! Technically speaking it seems that such a person could be elected as a proctor for the clergy but his position would be somewhat anomalous and so it is unlikely to occur in practice.

How representative is the house of bishops? It is surely right that every diocesan should be represented in the house of bishops *ex officio*, but questions arise with respect to the suffragans, who are far more numerous. At present the suffragans are treated as a definable interest group that ought to be represented as such in the Synod, and they elect some of their number to serve in that capacity. However, this means that some dioceses have two bishops in the Synod, and (theoretically at least) there is no reason why a diocese (like London, for example), should not end up with three or even more, depending on who is elected to serve. It must be admitted that to date the system has not been abused in that way but problems could arise and if they did, there would be nothing that anyone could do about them. Representation is also heavily weighted in favour of York, which elects four suffragans (from eleven dioceses) as compared to Canterbury, which has only five for thirty dioceses – proportionately half the number.[3]

Perhaps the best solution would be to admit the senior suffragan from each diocese. That would make election unnecessary, though it would also almost double the size of the house, something that would go against the drive for economy that has governed the pattern of Synod membership in recent years. Nevertheless, and especially in those places where suffragans have a defined geographical area that effectively functions as a kind of mini-diocese, a solution of that kind might be the fairest one. After all, if the dioceses concerned were to be formally subdivided into their respective areas, the suffragans would become diocesans and have an automatic entitlement to a seat in the Synod.

The problem of episcopal representation is compounded by the fact that in addition to the House of Bishops that is part of General Synod, there is a College of all the bishops, diocesan as well as suffragan, that meets on a regular basis and frames policy for the Church as a whole. The relationship between this College and the Synod is far from simple. In the 2012 debates over human sexuality, for example, the College of Bishops drafted a rather conservative statement that it then offered to

---

[3] York has twelve diocese but Sodor and Man does not count, because it has no suffragan.

Synod, expecting the latter to 'take note' of it – a sign of approval that falls short of outright adoption. But the liberals in the Synod managed to get it to vote according to houses, rather than as a single body, so instead of being 'noted' as it normally would have been, it was rejected in the house of clergy and the bishops were duly embarrassed. They went back to the drawing board, but it seems unlikely that they will modify their position to any great extent. Where this leaves the Church is unclear. Should the teaching authority of the episcopate be upheld, or can General Synod overrule that? Will the bishops seek to avoid a repeat performance by simply ignoring the Synod altogether, and if they do, what authority will their collective teaching have?

Another difficulty is that bishops are chosen by means that are far from democratic and do not necessarily reflect the views of the diocese. It is almost always the case that a diocesan bishop is appointed from elsewhere, and the criteria of selection may have little to do with the wishes of the diocese concerned. It is certainly true that the diocese is now consulted much more thoroughly than was the case in the past, but the perceived needs of the wider Church also play an important part in selection. Church officials want to preserve a balance between men and women, as well as representation from different strands of churchmanship, but this can cause problems of its own. Recently the suffragan bishop of Burnley (Philip North) was appointed to Sheffield, apparently with the approval of the diocesan representatives on the Crown Nominations Commission, but there was considerable opposition (much of it from outside the diocese) to him because he does not ordain women. Eventually he felt that he had to withdraw because he would not be able to unite the diocese behind him, and another candidate was appointed in his stead. In Blackburn diocese, the diocesan synod passed a resolution calling for liturgical provision to be made for transgendered people, even though the diocesan bishop, who is one of the most conservative on the bench, would almost certainly never have initiated such a move. Disconnects of these kinds call both synodical government and episcopacy into question – should the synod defer to the bishop, should the bishop conform to the synod, or should the anomaly be allowed to stand as part of the 'rich diversity' of the

Church of England? Whatever course is followed, it would appear that the integrity of the Church's administration is being called into question.

The house of clergy is elected by the licensed clergy of each diocese and numbers are determined by the size of the diocese. This represents a welcome change on the older system, in force before 1919, where there were two members of convocation for every diocese, large or small, who were elected by the beneficed clergy only. Not all the clergy take their duty to vote seriously and in some dioceses there can be difficulties in finding enough people willing to stand for election, but there can be little doubt that, of all the three houses, this one is the most truly representative of its constituency. The clergy vote for candidates who campaign among them and who are as representative of their electorate as they can reasonably be. Voters express a preference for as many candidates as there are places to fill, and the use of a multiple transferable voting system ensures that 'second-choice' candidates stand a reasonable chance of getting elected. There is no sense of a quota related to sex or churchmanship, so if the different constituencies that make up the Church are inadequately represented, the fault lies as much (if not more) with apathetic electors and/or absence of candidates as with the system itself.

There are, however, some anomalies that need to be recognised and possibly ironed out in a future revision of its membership. One of these is the residual representation of cathedral deans. This is now greatly reduced from the days when all deans sat in convocation along with an elected representative of the cathedral chapter in every diocese. The deans now elect only five of their number to represent them (three in Canterbury and two in York) and the chapters are ignored. The feeling is that cathedrals are a special interest category that ought to have a voice, though how effective it is may be questioned. They are too few in number to be genuinely representative of cathedrals as a whole and the General Synod has to look beyond them when legislating for cathedrals, as it has occasionally done. Whether that would change much (or at all) if the special representation of deans were to be abolished is doubtful, but their symbolic presence is thought to be useful, not least by the deans themselves, and so it is unlikely to disappear anytime soon.

That has not been the case with archdeacons, however. In the past they all sat in convocation, but after 1970 they were forced to elect representatives from among their number. That was abolished in 2005, and now archdeacons must stand for election alongside the other licensed clergy in the diocese. On the surface that may seem to be fair enough, but in practice archdeacons have an advantage since they do not have parochial responsibilities and in the nature of things they are better acquainted with the realities of diocesan life than most other clergy are. The result is that they tend to be elected when they stand, which has the effect of reducing the number of incumbents and other licensed clergy in the Synod. It is true that their numbers are limited to one per diocese (or electoral area in a large diocese like London), but that one stands a much higher than average chance of being elected than any other clergy candidate.

The house of clergy is also the repository of what remains of the special representation once accorded to the ancient 'peculiar jurisdictions'. Until recently, this was most obvious in the form of the university members, who were elected by the chaplains and other licensed clergy of the main universities in England. This has now been changed, in order to give representation to theological lecturers who are not university members, which is a considerable improvement, but further thought could be given to their role in the Synod. Are they there because they represent a special interest, or because they have expertise that is needed by the Synod as a whole? In this category may also be placed the special status accorded to chaplains in the armed forces, members of religious communities and other particular interest groups.[4] It is probably a good thing that their voice should be heard by the wider Church, but whether they should have the same voting rights as the diocesan clergy when they represent much smaller constituencies is more debatable. Here there is room for further reform, perhaps by

---

[4] If a representative of one of these groups is not ordained, he or she will sit in the house of laity.

granting such people some kind of non-voting observer status, but moves in that direction have been frustrated in the past and are unlikely to succeed in the foreseeable future.

Finally, there is the house of laity. Theoretically any lay person on the electoral roll of a parish church in England can stand for election to this house, but in practice very few do and those who stand are almost all members of a deanery synod. This is because they are not elected by everyone on the parish electoral rolls, but by the lay members of the deanery synods in each diocese, who themselves are a fairly unrepresentative group of lay people. Overall numbers are determined by the size of the electoral rolls in each diocese, so that those with a larger number of churchgoers will be represented accordingly. This seems reasonably fair in theory, though the fact that almost nobody on an electoral roll is aware that he or she is being used in this way detracts somewhat from the overall impression of equity. The directly elected members are supplemented by various officials like the Dean of the Arches, the vicars-general of each province, the three Church Estates Commissioners and the chairmen of bodies like the Central Board of Finance and the Pensions Board, assuming that they are laity.[1] There are also a number of co-opted members, though there is a limit for the total membership (including those elected by the dioceses), which is 136 for Canterbury and 59 for York.

Quite apart from anything else, most lay people have other occupations that make it difficult for them to do justice to Synod membership, with the result that those elected are usually people with time on their hands. Retired people and housewives are thus over-represented, whereas full-time employees are relatively few and far between. This is not to say that those elected do not take their responsibilities seriously. Many of them do and some are highly dedicated, but it is hard to claim that they are truly representative of their constituency. In the nature of things, it is often difficult to find people who are willing to stand and there is a

---

[5] If they are ordained, they sit in the house of clergy instead.

definite tendency for those with a particular agenda to put themselves forward and be elected because nobody else is available.

It is also the case that there is a greater tendency for members of the house of laity to be inadequately informed of the matters that they have to deal with, especially those that demand some knowledge of theology or church history. This is not their fault, of course, but several observers have noted that many of the debates in Synod are substandard because those who participate in them are unprepared and may be swayed by an appeal to the emotions rather than to reason. This problem is by no means absent from the other two houses, but at least bishops and clergy have received some kind of training in the disciplines with which they are called to deal, something that is much less true of the laity. Unfortunately, although the General Synod can debate theological questions and determine the Church's position on them, it is impossible to limit the voting to those who can claim to have some knowledge of the subject. At the same time, much synodical business is administrative in nature, and here the expertise of some lay members is often considerably greater than what is generally found in the other two houses. Is there any way that this can be formally recognised? Here there is a real weakness, but it is hard to see how it can be adequately addressed by a General Synod that is not, and cannot be, constituted in a way that would greatly reduce the problem, if not eliminate it altogether.

One feature common to both the house of clergy and the house of laity is that although the members are elected by the deanery synods there is no requirement that candidates must be members of them (or of a diocesan synod). There is less of a problem with this in the house of clergy since it is unusual for clerical electors to choose someone who is not one of their number, but it is more common in the house of laity. The result is that members of these two houses are not necessarily responsible to their electorates in any very direct way. Perhaps it would be better if the clergy and laity were chosen as delegates from deanery and diocesan synods which would ensure that they were members of them as well. That would narrow the pool of potential candidates for election, but would also ensure that those elected had to report back to their electors, and receive guidance from them, on a regular basis. The current system is too easily open to manipulation by special interest groups, some of which are highly organised and willing to exploit the apathy of people more closely connected to the grassroots who are reluctant to serve on yet another set of committees.

Competence

In principle, the General Synod can determine any matter that concerns the life of the Church of England, though in practice certain restrictions apply. All its decisions are subject to ratification by Parliament, following procedures laid down by statute which General Synod has no power to alter. Normally, Parliament gives effect to synodical decisions without serious debate, but that cannot be taken for granted, as the discussions surrounding the Churchwardens Measure (2001) demonstrated. If Synod were to vote to remove the queen as Supreme Governor of the Church for example, it would be exceeding its powers and presumably its proposal would be rejected by Parliament. Parliament also reserves the right to override or limit General Synod's actions if it chooses to do so. In 1998, for example, the Human Rights Act required all synodical measures, past and future, to be applied in a way that is consistent with the European Convention on Human Rights. This has not caused any problems so far, but as secular norms move ever further away from Christian principles, there is no telling how long this situation will last.

The potentially sinister implications of this uncertainty became more apparent in 2004, when the Civil Partnership Act provided 'that a Minister of the Crown may by order amend, repeal or revoke "Church legislation", a term defined so as to include Measures of the Church Assembly or General Synod and any orders, regulations, or other instruments made by virtue of such measures.'[1] As Chancellor Mark Hill has noted, 'reliance must be placed on the continuance of the constitutional convention that the government does not legislate for the

---

[6] M. Hill, *Ecclesiastical Law*, fourth edition (Oxford: Oxford University Press, 2018), p. 23, section 2.07.

Church of England without its consent.'[1] What that reliance is worth remains to be tested but the potential for conflict is there, not least in the realm of same-sex marriage, which was the context in which the provision was first articulated. It is by no means inconceivable that parliamentary pressure could be brought to bear on the Church if a sufficiently large and dedicated number of MP's was to determine that the Church is out of step with society in general and must be forced to come into line whether it wants to or not. Whether a European court could do the same is less clear, but the possibility must not be discounted.

It used to be thought by some that because historical formularies like the Thirty-nine Articles and the 1662 Book of Common Prayer (BCP) are protected by statute, that their status cannot be altered by synodical action, but this interpretation was rejected when it was challenged by Church Society following the ordination of women to the presbyterate, and it is now understood that not only do synodical measures, once they have been ratified by Parliament, have the force of law, but that they may relate to any matter involving the Church of England, including its historical doctrines and formularies.[2] There are special provisions for a two-thirds majority vote that must be honoured in such cases, but the matters themselves lie entirely within the competence of General Synod.

Any proposal that involves a change to the Church's official doctrine or authorised forms of worship must be referred to the house of bishops, who have the right to decide whether to proceed with it or not. If the bishops agree to take it forward, they must present it to the Synod in words of their own choosing, and the Synod cannot amend it. The houses of clergy and laity can, however, request a division, in which case the convocations of Canterbury and York vote separately. To be carried, the proposal must obtain a majority in both convocations, as well as in the house of bishops and the house of laity. If it fails in one of the convocations, it may be presented again and if it fails a second time, provision may be made for allowing it to pass with a two-thirds vote of

---

[7] Hill, *Ecclesiastical Law*, p. 23 (section 2.07).
[8] See Hill, *Ecclesiastical Law*, p. 11 (section 1.24).

both convocations sitting together. However, if the vote is lost in any one of the houses it fails and cannot be reintroduced within the lifetime of the synod in question.

Another restriction is that if a proposal involves changes to the sacraments or the Ordinal, it requires a two-thirds majority in all three houses. The same is true for any canon that touches on worship or doctrine. This requirement offers a degree of protection to significant minorities and ensures that important changes will not be made on the strength of wafer-thin majorities, but there is still scope left for dissent. That happened, for example, when the ordination of women to the presbyterate was approved by only two votes above the two-thirds threshold in the house of laity. The minority was strong enough and vocal enough in the wider Church to ensure that its dissent would continue, with the result that special provision has had to be made for them. More recently, the initial failure of the proposal to allow for the consecration of women as bishops led to 'facilitated conversations' orchestrated by professional mediators.[1] The only purpose of that was to ensure that the proposal would eventually pass, a fact that has led many to believe that 'facilitated conversations' are nothing more than a means of softening up the opposition. This ulterior motive may explain why, when a similar tactic was proposed as a way of resolving differences over the blessing of same-sex marriages, it was strongly resisted by those who thought that they were the intended targets of this technique.

One area in which the General Synod has virtually unlimited authority is that of canon law. The current canon law of the Church of England was overhauled in 1964-1969, when the ancient canons of 1604 were finally replaced. Most of them had fallen into disuse and some had become inapplicable, with the result that the whole subject had fallen into disrepute and little attention was paid to it. Since 1969 however, there has been a renascence of canon law in the Church of England and the canons have more bearing on church life than they had for centuries before then. Canon law revision was the work of the convocations, but

---

[9] See Hill, *Ecclesiastical Law*, pp. 31-32 (section 2.27) and especially note 93.

their powers were transferred to the General Synod which was constituted shortly after the new canons were promulgated. Over the past half century the Synod has introduced some far-reaching changes that have greatly affected parish life. Benefices have been united, new patterns of ministry have been developed and provisions designed to prevent such things as the sale of church offices (known as 'simony') have been scrapped as being no longer relevant.

In many cases, it must be admitted that the ongoing process of canon law development has been beneficial, though it is not without potential dangers that make take time to be fully revealed. The abolition of simony is a case in point. At the present time it is hard to see how church offices could be bought and sold, but any system is open to corruption and it may be unwise to remove provisions for dealing with that, especially when those provisions are of ancient origin. There is also a tendency towards centralisation that may yet turn out to have negative results in some instances.

One example of what can happen is the way in which the medieval dispute between the dean and chapter of Durham on the one hand, and the archbishop of York on the other, was eventually resolved. For centuries the dean and chapter had claimed (and exercised) the right to guard the spiritualities of the dioceses when there was a vacancy in the episcopal see. But the archbishops of York had always maintained that this right belonged to them – hence the dispute. One might have thought that it would have been resolved by accepting the actual situation and regularising the procedure by which the dean and chapter exercised this duty. But the amending canon passed in February 2000 put an end to the controversy by doing the opposite. It relieved all the deans and chapters of their historic responsibility and vested it in the two archbishops instead. In a sense therefore, the dispute was resolved in favour of York, though not directly, but as part of a wider reform. It is easy to see why resolving an ancient and somewhat ridiculous quarrel was a good thing, but whether centralised control was the best answer may be questioned. It was a bureaucratic decision designed for the convenience of administrators, which is symptomatic of the general trend in modern revision. Whether this will in turn produce new abuses of its own remains to be seen, but we must not be blind to the possibility that what looks like efficiency may turn out to have unforeseen problems of its own. General Synod's policy of 'one size fits all' has its attractions but it may end up removing safeguards that, however archaic they may have seemed at the time, nevertheless served a useful (if long dormant) purpose.

This modernisation process has not been without pain and not everyone is happy with every aspect of it, but on the whole it has been successful in its aims. What it has not done is reverse the decline of the Church overall, and in that sense it must be judged a failure. In the language of modern thought, General Synod has been good at maintenance but bad at mission. Ideally its success at the former ought to facilitate the latter, and that has certainly been the hope (and the claim) of those who have promoted change. But for whatever reason, the desired result has not materialised and it must be asked why that might be so. Have the expectations of Synod been too high? Is it capable of reaching out beyond itself and 'growing' the Church in new and unprecedented ways? Or is it the ultimate form of institutionalisation, capable of organising what is already there but unable to advance any further?

It is difficult to answer such questions because they touch on so many things that are imponderable. No synod can create faith, or ensure that the Holy Spirit will bring revival to dying churches and ministries. There is a constant danger that energy that ought to be spent in preaching the Gospel will instead be taken up by endless meetings whose purpose is unclear and whose results are meagre to non-existent. In fairness, General Synod has been alive to this danger and has responded to it by creating what has become known as the Simplification Task Group (STG), whose job is to make sure that the laws of the Church are both comprehensible and relevant to those who must obey them. But as we might expect, the STG can only apply bureaucratic remedies to what are essentially spiritual problems, with mixed results. On the one hand, it has succeeded in cleaning up a lot of useless and redundant legislation, which is undoubtedly a good thing, but at the same time it has sought to provide ways in which General Synod can act to achieve its aims without having to go through the difficult process of formal legislation. That this might lead to somewhat underhanded practices aimed at achieving results that would otherwise be frustrated is a danger that many have recognised, though what can (or should) be done about it is a question that has not (yet) been addressed. Only time will tell whether the proposed changes will work as they are intended to or not.

One example of the dilemma that faces the General Synod is in the way it approaches inter-church relations. It is possible for the Synod to legislate for what are known as 'local ecumenical projects', where clergy from different denominations work together in a framework of mutually-recognised ministry. But the same Synod cannot easily move from there to advancing wider church union because to do so would be to go beyond the boundaries set for it by law and introduce new complications. If union with the Methodists, for example, were to go ahead, what would happen to the Synod and the things that it administers? Would the Methodists have to merge into the Church of England, and if not, what role could the existing General Synod play in a united church? Would it have to be dissolved or reconstituted in a way that would make it something quite different from what it now is? The potential legal ramifications of church union would be considerable and it is most likely that, if such a situation were to occur, not only would a number of necessary changes be introduced but the opportunity would be taken to 'straighten out' other 'anomalies' otherwise unaffected by the union. Patronage rights, for example, might be an easy target and one not immediately apparent to those who are not directly affected by them.

This problem becomes even more acute when it comes to inter-church relations beyond England. Even within the Anglican Communion, it is hard to see how the Synod could accept oversight from a pan-Anglican body or subscribe to a mutually-agreed covenant, as the *Windsor Report* of 2004 suggested that it might. To be effective, an Anglican covenant would have to ensure that decisions taken at a Communion level would be applied by each local Anglican church, but whether the Church of England could promise to do that is unclear. The Synod cannot do anything that might compromise or diminish the sovereignty of Parliament, and as long as the Church of England remains established, Parliament is unlikely to agree to anything that would have that effect. As a result, although the General Synod might informally agree to apply Anglican Communion directives, there would be no compulsion on it to do so and if it chose not to, there is nothing that anyone could do about it.

What is true of the Anglican Communion is *a fortiori* true of the wider Christian world. It has been possible for the Synod to agree to mutual recognition of ministries with respect to other Protestant churches in Europe, but that is a very long way from formal union. To put it bluntly, the Church of England could not reunite with Rome even if it wanted to, because its constitutional structures stand in the way. In this sense it can even be argued that the creation of self-governing bodies within the Church has made such a prospect even less likely than it was before, because it adds an extra layer of bureaucracy that would-be ecumenists would have to overcome. There is certainly no prospect of Parliament ever agreeing to submit an established Church of the realm to a foreign jurisdiction (like that of the papacy), so any move in that direction is doomed from the start. The constraints on General Synod are more subtle and more far-reaching than many people realise at first sight.

In matters of doctrine, it might be theoretically possible for the General Synod to strike out in new directions but it is hard to see what it could really achieve by doing so. The historic formularies are protected by law and cannot be removed by synodical action alone. It might be possible for the Synod to authorise the use of church buildings by Muslims or other non-Christians, but that is controversial and it would certainly be impossible for it to adopt beliefs from another religion. Even the canonisation of Anglicans as 'saints' in the Roman Catholic sense is beyond its powers; the most that it can do is authorise the inclusion of worthy individuals in the church calendar. Widening the boundaries is virtually impossible, whatever may be theoretically conceivable on paper, so even if the Synod contains radical elements that want to move in that direction, achieving their aims is almost certainly more than can be expected.

In general, it can be said that General Synod would have considerable difficulty in trying to legislate on matters that by definition reach beyond the Church of England. It could not really change the canon of Scripture, for example, though it could mandate certain translations as more authoritative than others. It would have great difficulty in altering one of the ancient creeds, as a recent attempt to remove the *Filioque* clause from the Nicene Creed demonstrated. The intention was to bring the Creed into line with the Eastern Orthodox version but the consequent break with the rest of Western Christendom was too much, with the result that although the proposal passed the Synod, it was never implemented. It has successfully added, removed or altered saints' days in the calendar, but could not touch the major festivals – there is no prospect of it moving Christmas to July, for example, or fixing the date of Easter, even though it is technically within its competence to do so.

In these and many other respects, the General Synod effectively has to accept that the Church of England is not so autonomous as to be able to cut itself off from the rest of the Christian world, though where the boundaries lie is by no means always clear. This was demonstrated by its decision to approve the ordination of women to the presbyterate (priesthood) and now to the episcopate. It exercised its freedom to do so and acted in concert with some other Anglican provinces, as well as a number of other Protestant churches, but it went against both the Roman Catholic and Eastern Orthodox ones, a fact that was duly noted at the time and used by opponents of the move as an attempt to block it. The result was that some people left the Church of England on the ground that it was no longer 'catholic' because it had not accepted the consensus of the Christian world as a whole, and it must be admitted that the argument is not without some force. By acting as it did, the Church of England was effectively saying that it has the power to determine its own orders and that in consequence they are not automatically valid beyond its boundaries. Of course, Rome and the

Orthodox churches have said that all along so this comes as no surprise to them, but Anglicans have traditionally tried to have it both ways. By agreeing to the ordination and consecration of women, General Synod has rejected this claim to 'catholicity' and to that extent it has ensured that the ecumenical relations of the Church are unlikely to advance any further than they already have.

Another area where the competence of General Synod is effectively circumscribed by circumstances is that of churchmanship. The existence of well-defined Evangelical and Anglo-Catholic wings of the Church predates the creation of the Synod, but it can be argued that the revival of the convocations after 1852 was at least partly intended to prevent the rivalry between these groups (not to mention the 'Broad Church' middle ground) from splitting the Church apart. The different churchmanships entrenched themselves in the nineteenth century by creating theological colleges of their particular stripe and by purchasing or otherwise obtaining the advowsons to a number of benefices (livings) to which they could appoint men of their own choosing. The effects of this are still visible today and are largely responsible for the ongoing survival of forms of churchmanship that make the Church of England broader in practice than most other Anglican churches are. Officially speaking, General Synod has no brief in this area; there is no special provision made for representing particular forms of churchmanship (though the presence of representatives of the religious orders is obviously biased in favour of Anglo-Catholicism), even if both Evangelicals and Anglo-Catholics have informal subgroupings within the Synod that try to co-ordinate their activities and protect their interests.

But if General Synod is theoretically neutral in matters of churchmanship, in practice it tries to break down the barriers between them and (in the eyes of those who hold to particular positions on the matter) dilute what they stand for. This can be seen in Synod's attempts to regulate the curriculum and activities of the theological colleges, which are constantly being urged to become broader than they were originally intended to be. It can also be seen in the union of benefices, where patrons of a particular churchmanship are frequently forced to share their rights with others, which can easily have the effect of changing the identity of particular parishes. These activities can be justified in the name of co-ordinating resources, streamlining operations and even exposing people of certain convictions to other points of view so as to make them more tolerant and flexible, but whatever we may think of such aims, it is hard to deny that here is an area in which General Synod tries to alter the nature of the Church without declaring its intentions openly.

It is hardly surprising therefore that many Evangelicals and Anglo-Catholics (in particular) have come to regard it with great suspicion, and that those in the middle, many of whom are theologically liberal, have seized the opportunity to advance their own interests at the expense of what they perceive as the 'extremes' on either side. The reluctance of the two major churchmanship groups to act together, which is based on very real theological differences, makes it easier for the 'middle ground' to set the pace, and it is not difficult to see how it has effectively become the default position of the Church as a whole. There can be little doubt that the greater the autonomy of the General Synod becomes, the more it will move in this direction, to the detriment of vested churchmanship interests. Disestablishment, if it ever comes, would probably hasten this process, not least because the legal safeguards that continue to protect independent patronage would be abolished, as has happened in the disestablished Church in Wales. Already, bishops of one particular churchmanship are pressured into becoming broader in their outlook and the ordination of women has made it much harder for both Evangelicals and Anglo-Catholics to be appointed to senior positions in the Church. Admittedly, there are some who regret this narrowing of perspectives at the higher levels, but it is hard to avoid the impression that theirs are crocodile tears and that the movement towards the domination of an undifferentiated 'middle' is now unstoppable. In this process it must be said that General Synod has been a more active player than is generally admitted, and there is no reason to suppose that this will change anytime soon.

Consequences

The extension of General Synod's competence to cover all matters relating to the Church of England does not stop there. In practice, there are many other things that devolve to it, even though its responsibility for them is not specifically stated anywhere. This is especially true of matters that formally come under the bishops and could theoretically be exercised by them individually, but which are generally delegated to the Synod and its supporting bodies for the sake of consistency and efficiency.

This pattern is not new. In medieval times, bishops and even archdeacons had their own consistory courts, but over time these became moribund as legal rulings were increasingly the preserve of the Court of the Arches (in Canterbury) and the Auditor's Court (in York). Eventually these two courts were merged, creating the centralised ecclesiastical legal system that we know today.

It looks very much as though we may be witnessing a similar development with respect to General Synod today. Gradually, for reasons of convenience and consistency, the Synod is acquiring more and more responsibilities and making changes to the government of the Church of England that would have been inconceivable in earlier times. There is no reason to doubt that much of this work, perhaps most or even all of it, is a good thing and in some cases long overdue. But as institutions grow they take on more business and the procedures that were initially adequate become overburdened. When this happens, there is a push towards simplification, which means finding shortcuts to avoid the cumbersome processes that would normally be needed. Codes of practice, rules and conventions start to multiply in order to cope with the volume of material that has to be dealt with. As this happens, fewer and fewer people are directly involved in administration and only specialists (or those with time on their hands) can work it all out.

In the case of General Synod, the National Institutions Measure (1998) established the Archbishops' Council, with the express purpose of coordinating and furthering the work and mission of the Church of

England. The Council has a maximum of nineteen members, thirteen of whom are also members of General Synod.[1] The remaining six are appointed at the archbishops' discretion, but their appointments are subject to Synod's approval. This Council may be regarded as a standing committee of Synod and much of the Church's everyday administration is carried on by it, or by committees responsible to it. The Council submits an annual report to Synod before the July session and a report of its activities is given whenever Synod meets. This provides a degree of accountability, but in the nature of things it is clear that the Archbishops' Council is as important to Synod as the prime minister's cabinet is to Parliament.

The tendency to centralise and simplify is common to all institutions and General Synod cannot be singled out as being especially culpable in this respect. To a considerable extent, it relies on parliamentary precedent and practice, most of which is accepted by the public as fair, even if it is not widely understood. But General Synod differs from Parliament in the degree of accountability that its members have to the wider Church. The house of bishops, like the House of Lords, is a permanent fixture that is not subject to election, but unlike the Lords, the bishops have real powers and responsibilities. Who they are and how they are chosen matters in a way that is much less true of the peers of the realm and in some respects they can (and do) operate in ways that either bypass synodical procedures entirely or else control them to a substantial degree. The house of clergy is reasonably accountable to the licensed diocesan clergy since most of the proctors belong to their own diocesan synod where all the clergy are represented, but the same is not necessarily true of the house of laity.

It has to be admitted that the house of laity has major problems of credibility that seem to defy resolution. It has never been entirely clear who the 'laity' of the Church of England are, but even if we accept that

---

[10] They are the prolocutors of the two convocations, the chairman and vice-chairman of the house of laity and two delegates from each of the three houses, along with the two archbishops who act as joint presidents and one of the Church Estates Commissioners.

they can only really be those whose names are on parish electoral rolls, there is little or no contact between parishioners and those who supposedly represent them. It is quite possible to be a lay member of a parish without having any sort of contact with the lay representatives in General Synod, who are elected not by them, but by the lay members of the deanery synods of each diocese. Only by becoming a member of a deanery synod is it possible for a lay person to have any say at all in the election of the house of laity, and even the many of the candidates who put themselves forward will be virtually unknown to most of the electors. It is true that they usually put out campaign manifestos which give some idea of what they stand for but they never seek wider approval for the way they vote. A member of synod can do more or less whatever he or she pleases without fear of interference from the electorate.

The root of the problem seems to be that General Synod borrows parliamentary practices and procedures to give it the appearance of a democracy, but in reality it operates quite differently. Its leadership is not elected in any meaningful sense and the composition of its houses only partly (and often quite inadequately) reflects the reality of the Church on the ground. Most lay people, for example, are only barely aware of its existence and have no idea that they are represented in it because they are never given a chance to vote for the people who are supposed to represent them. The system works in favour of special interest groups and activists with their own agendas, which may be a long way from what the ordinary person in the pew understands or accepts.

Rightly or wrongly, General Synod is remote from the lives of most churchgoers, and yet it has great (and increasing) power to affect the way they worship. Everything from liturgy to the standards required of the clergy and even the maintenance of the property comes within its remit, and although the practical effects of this may appear to be slight, over time they can accumulate and produce a Church of England quite different from the one that we have become accustomed to. That changes should occur is inevitable and many of them may be both uncontroversial and beneficial, but it is the principle that counts, and at that level it must be concluded that the Church is being governed by mechanisms that give an appearance of consultation, and even of democracy, but that in reality are insulated from the lives of most parishioners. If there are some exceptions to this general picture, it is almost certainly because the local clergy are alert to what is going on and can stir up their congregations, but that is rare and the likely effect will be minimal because few people outside the parish concerned will have any knowledge of what is going on there, and probably not much interest in it either. The sad fact is that, despite the best of intentions, General Synod is not as representative a body as it ought to be, and correcting this 'democratic deficit' may be virtually impossible within the present system. Whether it is wise, given these circumstances, for such wide-ranging powers to be entrusted to the Synod may be doubted, but as there is unlikely to be any significant change to the current procedures in the foreseeable future, concerned members of the Church of England must be alert to the danger and do what they can to monitor the situation.

4. OTHER SYNODS

Diocesan synods

The attention that is focused on General Synod makes it easy to forget that it is part of a wider synodical structure that is designed to broaden decision-making in the Church and to devolve certain matters to levels at which they can be handled more effectively. The disappearance of provincial synods has been compensated for by a revival of diocesan ones instead. This may be regarded as belated recognition that dioceses have grown in importance since the early nineteenth century, but we should be careful not to exaggerate this. It is true that there has been a great increase in the number of dioceses since 1836, when reforms were first proposed, and that the enormous and unwieldy ones of the past (London, Lincoln, Exeter and York, to name but four of the most extreme) have been broken up into more manageable units. There are signs however that this trend may be coming to an end, as the recent amalgamation of three northern dioceses (Ripon, Wakefield and Bradford) into the new diocese of Leeds suggests. Nowadays, it seems that there is a preference for large dioceses to be subdivided into episcopal areas, presided over by suffragans, rather than to split them off to become independent dioceses in their own right.

Whatever the case may prove to be in the longer term, there is no doubt that diocesan synods are closer to the grassroots of the Church than the General Synod is, or can be. Each of them is presided over by its diocesan bishop and the suffragans are fully represented in them. Clergy and laity are also elected in roughly equal numbers by the deanery synods. Every deanery elects at least two clergy and two laity, bu these numbers may be increased to reflect the size of the deanery in question. Every diocesan synod must have at least 150 but not more than 270 members in all, including co-opted and *ex officio* ones. This is an important constraint, because there is a generous supply of *ex officio* members that includes all those who have been elected to General Synod. This ensures that there is a real connection between General Synod and the dioceses, but such members are deputised by the General Synod and not the other way round. It is therefore possible to fail to be elected to a diocesan synod but nevertheless to sit in it by virtue of belonging to General Synod. That situation is doubtless rare, but it is possible and must be regarded as a potential source of weakness. It is also possible for a diocesan synod to be subdivided into area synods where a diocese is so subdivided, making it more difficult to decide what 'approval by a diocesan synod' actually means.

Diocesan synod elections take place every three years, which puts them out of line with General Synod, which is elected only every five. This means that casual vacancies can easily occur among the *ex officio* members, though the places are automatically filled by their successors. Any elected member of the synod who leaves the diocese must vacate his or her seat, which is then filled by a by-election if there is more than nine months to go before the next general election is called. Given the relatively short interval of three years between general elections, this provision reduces the number of casual vacancies that need to be filled and those so elected will serve for only a short time. In general therefore, membership of diocesan synods is likely to experience a higher turnover than in General Synod, which in turn means that the membership will probably be less experienced and less able to make an effective contribution to the running of the diocese.

This is important because diocesan synods are more active than most people imagine. In matters relating to forms of worship and relations with other Christian bodies, approval from a majority of diocesan synods is required before any alterations or modifications to the existing pattern can be introduced. Diocesan synods must also approve the diocesan budget and oversee a wide range of subordinate committees and agencies, including ones for mission, education and patronage. Because of this, their impact on parish life may be considerably greater than the actions of General Synod, though relatively few people seem to be aware of this.

Diocesan synods may advise the bishop on matters of policy and make suggestions for the General Synod to consider, as the diocesan synod of Blackburn recently did when it requested a discussion of provision for the transgendered. Usually however, this function is delegated to the bishop's council or to the standing committee of the diocese, both of which must be constituted by law. On the other hand, a diocesan synod has no authority to pronounce on any matter of doctrine and it must keep the deanery synods properly informed of its activities, making it at least partially accountable to the lower tier of synods.

Deanery synods

Below the diocesan synods are those of the deaneries, into which every diocese (except Sodor and Man) is subdivided.[1] These synods are presided over by the rural (or area) dean and a chairman elected by the lay representatives. To some extent, they fulfil the functions previously exercised by the rural dean on his own, though their powers are considerably greater than that. Membership of the deanery house of clergy is given to all licensed clergy resident in the deanery and is even open to retired clergy, who may elect one for every ten of them who are so resident. The house of laity is elected by the parochial church councils in every parish, and their numbers are determined in such a way as to ensure that they are at least as numerous as the clergy. In principle a deanery synod must have at least fifty but not more than 150 members, though the figure may be higher if the house of laity has to be expanded in order to equal the size of the house of clergy. There are the usual provisions for *ex officio* members to be appointed and for additional clergy to be co-opted, though the latter must not exceed five percent of the total. Because local circumstances vary a good deal, there is more flexibility in the composition of deanery synods than there is with the others, and the rules governing vacancies are less rigid. It is possible for both lay people and clergy to continue as members of a deanery synod after their entitlement to be there has expired, though there is a kind of honour system that is supposed to ensure that those who cease to be qualified should vacate their seats. As with diocesan synods, elections are held every three years and casual vacancies are filled by the relevant parochial church councils.

---

[1] Sodor and Man had four deaneries in the past but these have now been amalgamated.

Other Synods

Diocesan synods may delegate some of their responsibilities to the deaneries, notably the fixing of the 'parish share' or quota payable to the diocese, but beyond that, their functions are rather vaguely defined in terms such as 'promoting a spirit of fellowship in the deanery', whatever that might mean in practice. Now that benefices are increasingly united in various schemes of group and team ministries the task of co-ordination is often left to the group or team in question. Some of these can be almost as large as a deanery, making this activity somewhat redundant at deanery level but (probably) ensuring greater practical effectiveness in the group or team concerned.

Deanery synods act as sounding boards for the diocese and are supposed to allow for grassroots opinion in the Church to be heard at the higher levels, though how well this functions is open to question. What does matter is that deanery synods elect members of the diocesan synod and in the case of the laity, of General Synod as well. This is a fairly distant power, exercised only once every five years in the case of General Synod, but it is not unimportant.

The biggest problem with deanery synods is lack of interest at parochial level, especially among the laity. The clergy belong to it whether they attend the meetings or not (and many are far from regular at this) but lay people have to be selected and it is often difficult to find anyone willing to serve. It is impossible to generalise, but there is a widespread feeling that most of the lay members have been persuaded by their clergy to put themselves forward, and the PCC is often only too glad to let such 'volunteers' represent them. Here there is a real weakness in the system that it seems almost impossible to address. Rightly or wrongly, most parishioners have not become enthusiastic about synodical government, and it is at this most basic level that their disinterest stands out for all to see.

Ironically perhaps, it is at the deanery level that the utility of regular synods is likely to be questioned the most. Do we really need them? Diocesan synods make sense and have real responsibilities, even if they are not appreciated as much as they ought to be, but is anything to be gained by pushing subsidiarity (as the delegation of powers is called) to a more local level? And if there is, do we really need a body that consists of fifty people *as a minimum* and perhaps three times as many as that, in order to meet this need? Here are questions worth asking – and answering – in ways that do more than simply try to justify the *status quo*.

5. Challenges for the Future

Is synodical government as presently constituted in the Church of England the best way of handling ecclesiastical business? The question was asked a few years after the inauguration of the General Synod and a series of essays was published on the subject in 1986, but since that time there does not seem to have been much thought given to the appropriateness of the basic principle.[1] It is safe to assume that, although there are periodic suggestions for tinkering with the existing structure and some reforms have been enacted, synodical government is here to stay for the foreseeable future. It therefore seems that the most practical course for us to adopt is to accept this reality and suggest further ways in which 'tinkering' could be explored in order to make the system more practical and serviceable in the life of the Church.

Composition

The Church has paid considerable attention to ways in which the General Synod's membership can be slimmed down, the main object of this being to save money. Some useful reforms have been made, but there is scope for a more comprehensive approach. In this essay we have suggested that the House of Bishops could be enlarged to include a suffragan from very diocese that has them. Suffragans would no longer be seen as a particular constituency that sends its own elected representatives to Synod but as an integral part of the various dioceses, giving them a more meaningful role and making it easier for them to stand in for the diocesan when required, or when the see is vacant. The practical effect of this would be to enlarge the House of Bishops by about thirty members, but this inflation of numbers could be compensated for by reducing the size of the other two houses.

The House of Clergy could dispense with the remnants of the 'peculiar jurisdictions' of old, with a proviso that when matters concerning them are being discussed, they should be fully consulted. Deans of cathedrals, for example, could be summoned when the administration of cathedrals

---

[1] Peter Moore, ed., *The synod of Westminster: do we need it?* (London: SPCK, 1986).

is being considered, and it ought to be possible to ensure that consent from a significant number of them would be required before any measure affecting them directly is passed. Similar considerations could be applied to the different chaplaincies and religious orders, so that their special interests would be protected. This would also affect the House of Laity to some extent, since non-ordained representatives of these special jurisdictions sit in it rather than in the House of Clergy.

Diocesan synods seem to be about right in the way that they are composed, but a case could surely be made for elevating area synods in the larger dioceses to the same status and abolishing deanery synods altogether. Once again, it ought to be possible to ensure that when desirable, a diocesan synod could be broken down into deaneries for particular purposes, but there seems to be little justification for keeping an entire level of government in existence when so much of what it does replicates what is (or can be) done elsewhere. Parishes could be entitled to delegate members of the diocesan synod according to a system of weighting that would allow some representation from everyone but give a greater say to larger congregations. It could also be stated that those parishes who fail to pay their way would lose their voting rights in the synod. They should not be silenced altogether, but defaulters should suffer some penalty, and this would seem to be an appropriate one to impose on them.

Competence

The restrictions currently in place with respect to the competence of diocesan synods should be maintained, but there is scope for clarifying the remit of General Synod, which appears to be too broad. When synodical government was established in 1970 it was assumed that it would not legislate on matters that would affect the basic identity of the Church of England as a Christian body, and so far, it is fair to say, those boundaries have been respected in practice. General Synod could theoretically drop the Bible or the doctrine of the Trinity, for example, though nobody has gone that far – at least not yet.

No doubt many people will think that it is alarmist to imagine a scenario in which such fundamental features of the Church were called into question, but we must not be too sanguine about this. There were thinkers in the eighteenth century who would happily have dispensed with Trinitarian doctrine, for example, and given the general ignorance on the subject, it is not inconceivable that the matter could be raised again, perhaps in the context of 'inter-faith dialogue'. Why place barriers in the way of co-operation between Christians on the one hand, and Jews or Muslims on the other, it might be argued, and if the 'common monotheism' of the Abrahamic faiths were to be given official recognition, the doctrine of the Trinity would presumably have to be sacrificed in the process.

That might seem unlikely right now, but it could happen. A generation ago nobody thought that the Church of England would open its orders to women, still less that it would consider what should be done about same-sex marriage. There appears to be a general consensus at the present time that matters like these are of secondary importance and do not touch on fundamental points of doctrine, but that assumption can be contested, and indeed it has been by some who have felt compelled to leave the Church because they believe that the General Synod has acted *ultra vires*. Legal opinion has not supported them in this, but that in itself makes clarification more desirable. Where does the boundary between fundamental ('first order') and secondary ('second order') issues lie, and is there any way in which the competence of General Synod can be restricted to the latter? Relying on common sense and a widespread respect for tradition may be a good start, but is it enough? It is fair to say that doubts on this score are growing, and urgent clarification is needed to prevent the Synod from diluting the character of the Church by legislating in ways that go against the traditional consensus of the wider Christian world.

In particular, matters of doctrine should not be decided by General Synod alone. Many of its members have no competence in the field and even those with degrees in theology may find it difficult to follow some of the more complex debates. Many points of doctrine seem obscure when considered in isolation, and the temptation to ignore them, or to modify them may increase accordingly. It is quite alarming to think that no consultation with professional opinion is required before making such changes. Of course, expert advice is not infallible and the Church cannot submit itself to what could easily become a tyranny of its own, but to debate the removal of the *Filioque* clause from the Nicene Creed (for example) without understanding much about it is surely taking things too far in the opposite direction. Perhaps the only practical way forward here is to recognise that there are many questions that have far-reaching implications that a Synod of one particular Church cannot really decide on its own. Article 21 of the Thirty-nine Articles of Religion envisaged the continuance of General Councils of the wider church, though it was quick to specify that even those councils were not infallible. That may be true, but it is still better to refer (and defer) to them in matters that will affect Christians beyond the bounds of the Church of England and not take the law into our own hands.

Many people think that Synod's decision-making process is too slow and cumbersome, which in some respects it is, but when it comes to matters of major and far-reaching importance, it can equally well be argued that the process is not slow enough. If General Synod could be revamped along the lines suggested here, the pattern of voting could also be adjusted to ensure that when changes are proposed, there is a genuine consensus for them. For example, the current requirements for qualified majorities in the Synod could be maintained but supplemented by a ratification process that would require similar majorities in *all* the diocesan synods.[1] That would take time, but it would guarantee that there would be general agreement across the Church and perhaps obviate the need for special arrangements (like the so-called 'flying bishops') that proliferate when a minority opinion is too strong to be ignored. This may seem 'undemocratic' to some, but the Church is not a parliamentary democracy in which the majority rules; it is a fellowship of believers who should be in agreement as far as is humanly possible. The spirit that should guide us is the one that led the Apostle

---

[2] On matters relating to the laws of England alone, the dioceses of Sodor and Man and of Gibraltar might be excepted.

Paul, when speaking about the consumption of meat that had been sacrificed to idols, wrote: '...sinning against your brothers and wounding their conscience when it is weak, you sin against Christ. Therefore, if food makes my brother stumble, I will never eat meat, lest I make my brother stumble (1 Corinthians 8:12-13).'

Consequences

The ongoing problem, of course, is trying to decide how to ensure that General Synod stays within the boundaries traditionally recognised as 'Christian' and consonant with the Western theological tradition as the Church of England has received it. This is not to impugn the integrity of the Eastern tradition, but simply to ensure that if modifications are to be made that they cohere with the wider body of received teaching that we share with others who think they way we do. For example, the Eastern churches have never pronounced on the doctrine of justification by faith alone, at least partly because the concept of justification and the way it has been interpreted in both Protestant and Roman Catholic traditions, is alien to their theology. That is clearly a problem for ecumenical dialogue to sort out, but the Church of England cannot follow the argument that because there is a substantial body of Christians that has been unable to accept teaching that does not fit into their way of thinking we should drop our own position on the subject. Justification by faith alone makes sense in our context, and to remove it from our theology would be to render it both incoherent and unorthodox. Yet General Synod is empowered to do just that if it puts its mind to it!

In addressing this issue the Church of England has to work within the constraints of its established status. Parliamentary sovereignty does not allow it to submit in any formal way to an external body, whether that is the jurisdiction of Rome, the World Council of Churches or even the Anglican Communion. Yet the events of the past generation, and in particular the pending disintegration of the Anglican Communion for want of an agreed process for establishing its common identity, make the case for some kind of wider accountability on the part of individual churches. In this respect, the Church of England is no different from any other, even if the way in which it declares its adherence to a more universal body must be expressed according to its own constitution. Probably the only way that this can be done at present is by voluntary restraint. General Synod ought to declare that there are some subjects on which it will not pronounce, even if it has the juridical competence to do so. This would include such things as the canon of Scripture, the content and authority of the Creeds and even (at a very different level) the dates of Christmas and Easter. We may be legally sovereign, but we still have a responsibility to walk as far as we can together with our fellow Christians who live in other contexts.

In the nature of the case, General Synod ought to declare that it will not go against the consensus of the Anglican Communion on matters that bind us together and create our identity in the broader Christian world. It should also be understood that we will not question the foundational elements of our faith as expressed in the Thirty-nine Articles of Religion and the other formularies of our Church. To the objection that the Articles legislate on matters that pertain *only* to England, and that some of them are now outdated, it can be objected that they are set out in a descending order of importance and can be dealt with accordingly. Articles 1-8 are 'catholic' in the traditional sense, Articles 9-34 are Protestant, Articles 35-37 are specific to the Church of England and Articles 38 and 39 form an appendix which, like Articles 1-8, is of universal application. Thus, it would be possible for the Synod to alter the provisions of Articles 35-37, which lie within its competence, but not the others – at least not without consulting other Christian churches and seeking consensus with them. We should not expect the Roman Church to agree with Articles 9-34, but 1-8 and 38-39 apply to it as much as to anyone else. If an approach like this could be adopted and expressed in a written statement of some kind that would underscore its importance, there is at least a chance that the Synod would be constrained to remain within certain well-defined and generally accepted boundaries, and that there would be no danger that we would suddenly wake up to find that we have suddenly become Unitarians (for example) by virtue of a narrow vote in General Synod.

Some of this will doubtless seem far-fetched, but it is precisely when the likelihood of such developments is doubtful that the possibility of their occurring needs to be countered. If we wait for them to arise, the Church will find itself in crisis and the latter state will be worse than the first.

In conclusion, therefore, we may say that synodical government, like any system, has its strengths and its weaknesses. For better or for worse, we have now inherited it and are unlikely to see it disappear anytime soon. What we need to do therefore, instead of criticising it or ignoring it as far as we can, is to tweak it in ways that will improve its ability to function and at the same time restrain it from doing things that will call the wider unity and Christian integrity of the Church into question. If we think like that and proceed accordingly, there is a good chance that we can make our current system of synodical government work as it ought to and that our missionary vocation in the world will be enhanced, not compromised.

6. Evangelicals and Synodical Government

It is generally accepted that Evangelicals in the Church of England punch below their weight in its synodical and administrative structures. To some extent this may reflect a certain institutional bias against them, but the problem is not nearly as simple as that. The fact is that for most of the past century, Evangelicals have paid little attention to the Church's increasing self-government and have failed to take full advantage of the opportunities available to them. The parochial system has encouraged parochialism, and many Evangelicals would rather preach and evangelise at the local level than involve themselves in wider affairs that seem to have little relevance to them. For a long time that attitude was understandable and could be justified, but that is no longer the case. Recent events have made it clear that General Synod (in particular) and its subsidiary bodies are governing the Church much more than they ever did in the past, and the traditional isolationism is no longer an option. What should be done about this?

First of all, Evangelicals must overcome their aversion to politics. We believe in the power of prayer, but we also have a system of government that requires participation, and 'praying about it' is not enough. Evangelical clergy need to be sensitised to the need for them to get involved, and to encourage their parishioners to do the same. There are many good people who are able and might be persuaded to serve if the importance of what they are being asked to do were made plain to them. Evangelicals are good at organising conferences – why not have one devoted to this theme? Church government needs to be seen as a mission field, and one that has potentially wide implications for the evangelisation of the nation. Putting the right people with the right priorities in the right positions is a key ministry in itself, and if places in Synod go to unsuitable candidates more or less by default, we must step up and do what we can to change that.

Secondly, Evangelicals must have the right priorities and be prepared to form alliances with others who share them. In a world where same-sex marriage threatens the integrity of our society, arguing over liturgical niceties is a luxury that we can ill afford. This is not to say that such things are unimportant – we should not be forced to wear stoles or to pray for the dead and ought to resist attempts to make matters of that kind the expected norm. But we must also look beyond these concerns to the greater threats that assail us, and seek to persuade those who might disagree with us on some things to unite in pursuit of more important aims. This is not a matter of compromise but of leadership, and there has never been a time when good leaders have bene in shorter supply.

Evangelicals must do more to inform their congregations of what is going on in the wider Church and persuade them to support the creation of a cohort of specialists who can articulate the Church's doctrine and work to reform its discipline from within. The work of the Latimer Trust is of vital importance, but how many people know of its existence or understand what it is doing? Why are so many people 'too busy' to get involved in something that has the potential to influence the future direction of the Church for years to come?

There is no quick fix solution here. We need young people who are prepared to meet the challenge of serving in Church administration and government, who will see their commitment to synods and committees as a form of evangelism and who will put themselves forward for election in 2020, 2025, 2030 and so on. These people need to be recruited, but they also need to be resourced, and here the assistance of Evangelical societies is essential. They have the vision needed to establish priorities, organise candidates and voting, and give people a sense of what needs to be done. For better or for worse, the synods are here to stay and they will almost certainly become more powerful in years to come. Evangelicals must accept that and prepare themselves to play their part in shaping the mission to the nation that we all so much desire to support.

Recently Released by the Latimer Trust
Lex Orandi, Lex Credendi by *Martin Davie*

The Latin phrase lex orandi, lex credendi ('the law of praying is the law of believing') is a phrase which is often used in Anglican theological discussion, but which needs careful unpacking if its meaning is to be properly understood.

In this study Martin Davie provides such unpacking. He traces the history of the phrase back to its origins in the work of St. Prosper of Aquitaine in the fifth century, explains what it means and gives examples of how it has been both used and misused in the Roman Catholic, Orthodox and Anglican traditions.

His conclusion is that when it is rightly understood the principle lex orandi, lex credendi provides a useful tool for assessing both a church's liturgy and its doctrine. It reminds us that a church's liturgical practice needs to cohere with its doctrine and both need to be in line with Scripture.

He also argues that the use of this tool shows us that not only are proposals for marking same-sex relationships unacceptable, but so also is the new proposal to use liturgy to mark gender transition.

Anglican Elders by *Ed Moll*

Plural eldership and Anglican polity have long been held to be incompatible. Anglicans have inherited a sole presybterate as the normal pattern for congregational leadership, yet faithfulness to the patterns of leadership described in the New Testament lead evangelicals to look for ways to share ministry and leadership locally. The 'one-man band' model of ministry is simply not biblical. It is also not psychologically sustainable in the face of the growing demands of pastoral leadership. Plural leadership is desirable, but how can it be reconciled to Anglican polity?

This study explores the biblical and historical background to locally shared pastoral leadership within an Anglican context. It goes on to describe the experience of nine UK Anglican pastors who have established a pastoral leadership team that functions as a plural eldership. Practical lessons are drawn for today's church, with a particular focus on how this model enhances the church's ministry of making disciples.

Anglican Foundations Series

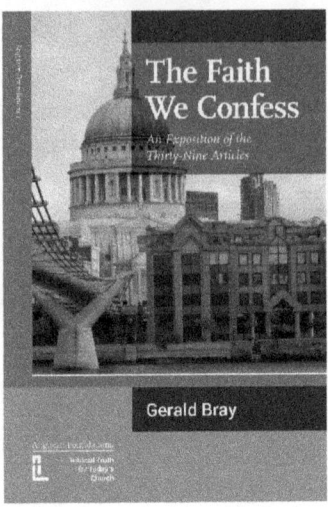

The Anglican Foundations series are a collection of books which offer practical guidance on Church of England services.

These include:
- The Faith We Confess – An exposition of the Thirty-Nine Articles
- The 'Very Pure Word of God – The Book of Common Prayer as a model of biblical liturgy
- Dearly Beloved – Building God's people through morning and evening prayer
- Day by Day – The rhythm of the Bible in the Book of Common Prayer
- The Supper – Cranmer and Communion
- A Fruitful Exhortation – A guide to the Homilies
- Instruction in the Way of the Lord – A guide to the catechism
- Till Death Do Us Part – "The solemnization of Matrimony" in the Book of Common Prayer
- Sure and Certain Hope – Death and burial

www.ingramcontent.com/pod-product-compliance
Lightning Source LLC
Chambersburg PA
CBHW031500040426
42444CB00007B/1155